THE
HISTORICAL ROLE OF ISLAM

THE HISTORICAL ROLE OF ISLAM

(An Essay on Islamic Culture)

By

M. N. Roy

GYAN

Published by

GYAN

Gyan Publishing House
5, Ansari Road
Daryaganj, New Delhi-110002
Phone: 011-47034999, 9811692060
E-mail: books@gyanbooks.com

Distribution Network
gyanbooks.com
India, USA, Canada, UK, Australia

ISBN: 978-93-6208-559-7 (HB)
First Published, 1937

2nd Impression 2024

Printed at: Gyan Press, Delhi.

THE HISTORICAL ROLE OF ISLAM
Author: M. N. ROY

THE HISTORICAL ROLE OF ISLAM

The phenomenal success of Islam was primarily due to its revolutionary significance and its ability to lead the masses out of the hopeless situation created by the decay of antique civilisations not only of Greece and Rome but of Persia and China and of India.'

The sword of Islam, wielded ostensibly at the service of God, actually contributed to the victory of a new social force—the blossoming of a new intellectual life which eventually dug the graves of all religions and faiths.'

The spirit of Islam was not invented by the genius of Mohammad; nor was it revealed to him. It was a heritage of history conferred on the Arabian nation. The greatness of Mohammad was his ability to recognise the value of the heritage and make his countrymen conscious of it.'

M. N. ROY.

THE

HISTORICAL ROLE OF ISLAM

(An Essay on Islamic Culture).

BY

M. N. ROY

VORA & Co. PUBLISHERS Ltd.

8, ROUND BUILDING BOMBAY 2.

CONTENTS.

CHAPTER ONE.

INTRODUCTION.

THE apparently sudden rise and the dramatic expansion of Mohammedanism constitutes a most fascinating chapter in the history of mankind. A dispassionate study of this chapter is of great importance in the present fateful period of the history of India. The scientific value of the study by itself is great, and the meritorious quest for knowledge is sure to be handsomely rewarded. But with us, to-day in India, particularly with the Hindu, a proper understanding of the historical role of Islam and the contribution it has made to human culture has acquired a supreme political importance.

This country has become the home of a very considerable number of the followers of the Arabian Prophet. One seldom realises that many more Mohammedans live in India than in any single purely Islamic country. Still, after the lapse of many centuries, this numerous section of the Indian population is generally considered to be an extranuous element. This curious but extremely regrettable cleft in the loose national structure of India has its historical cause. The Mohammedans originally came to India as invaders. They conquered the country and became its rulers for several hundred years. That relation of the conqueror and the subjugated has left its mark on the history of our nation which to-day embraces the both. But the unpleasant memory of the past relation has been progressively eclipsed by the present companionship in slavery. The effect of British Imperialism is no less painful and ruinous for the bulk of the Muslim population than for the masses professing Hinduism. So completely have the Mohammedans become an integral part of the Indian nation that the annals of the Muslim rule are justly recorded as chapters of the history of India. Indeed, Nationalism has gone farther in effacing the painful memory of the past.

The practice of seeking consolation for the shame of the present in the real or legendary glory of the past has dressed the

Muslim rulers of India in brilliant national colours.

Yet, a Hindu, who prides in the prosperity of the reign of an Akbar, or boasts of the architectural accomplishments of a Shah-jehan, is even to-day separated most curiously by an unbridgeable gulf from his next door neighbour belonging to the race, or professing the faith, of those illustrious monarchs who are believed to have glorified the history of India. For the orthodox Hindus who constitute the great majority of the Indian population, the Mussulman, even of a noble birth or high education or admirable cultural attainments, is a '*mlechha*'—impure barbarian—who does not deserve a social treatment any better than accorded to the lowest of the Hindus.

The cause of this singular situation is to be traced in the prejudice born, in the past, of the hatred a conquered and oppressed people naturally entertained for the foreign invader. The political relation out of which it sprang is a thing of the past. But the prejudice still persists not only as an effective obstacle to national cohesion, but also as a hindrance for a dispassionate view of history. Indeed, there is no other example of two communities living together in the same country for so many hundred years, and yet having so little appreciation of each other's culture. No civilised people in the world is so ignorant of Islamic history and contemptuous of the Mohammedan religion as the Hindus. Spiritual imperialism is the outstanding feature of our nationalist ideology. But this nasty spirit is the most pronounced in relation to Mohammedanism. The current notion of the teachings of the Arabian Prophet is extremely ill-informed. The average educated Hindu has little knowledge of, and no appreciation for, the immense revolutionary significance of Islam, and the great cultural consequences of that revolution. The prevailing notions could be laughed at as ridiculous, were they not so pregnant with harmful consequences. These notions should be combatted for the sake of the national cohesion of the Indian people as well as in the interest of science and historical truth. A proper appreciation of the cultural significance of Islam is of supreme importance in this crucial period of the history of India.

The great historian Gibbon describes the rise and expansion of Islam as "one of the most memorable revolutions which has impressed a new and lasting character on the nations of the globe." One is simply amazed to contemplate the incredible rapidity with which the two mightiest empires of the ancient time were subverted by the comparatively small bands of nomads issuing from the Arabian desert, fired with the zeal of a new faith. Hardly fifty years had passed since Mohammad assumed the role of the singular Prophet spreading his Message of Peace at the point of the sword, his followers victoriously planted the banner of Islam on the confines of India, on the one side, and on the shore of the Atlantic, on the other. The first Khalifs of Damascus reigned over an Empire which could not be crossed in less than five months on the fleetest camel. At the end of the first century of the Hegira, the "Commanders of the Faithful" were the most powerful rulers of the world.

Every prophet establishes his pretension by the performance of miracles. On that token, Mohammad must be recognised as by far the greatest of all prophets, before or after him. The expansion of Islam is the most miraculous of all miracles. The Roman Empire of Augustus, as later enlarged by the valiant Trajan, was the result of great and glorious victories, won over a period of seven hundred years. Still, it had not attained the proportions of the Arabian Empire established in less than a century. The

Empire of Alexander represented but a fraction of the vast domain of the Khalifs. For nearly a thousand years, the Persian Empire resisted the arms of Rome, only to be subdued by the "Sword of God" in less than a decade. Let a modern historian describe the miracle of the rise of Islam.

"Nowhere was there a vestige of an Arabian state, of a regular army, or of a common political ambition. The Arabs were poets, dreamers, fighters, traders; they were not politicians. Nor had they found in religion a stablising or unifying power. They practised a low form of polytheism...... A hundred years later, these obscure savages had achieved for themselves a great world power. They had conquered Syria and Egypt, they had overwhelmed and converted Persia, mastered Western Turkestan and part of the Punjab. They had wrested Africa from the Byzantines and the Berbers, Spain from the Visigoths. In the West they threatened France, in the East Constantinople. Their fleets, built in Alexandria or the Syrian ports, rode the waters of the Mediterranean, pillaged the Greek islands and challenged the naval power of the Byzantine Empire. Their success had been won so easily, the Persians and Berbers of the Atlas Mountains alone offering a serious resistance, that at the beginning of the eighth century it must have seemed an open question whether any final obstacle could be opposed to their victorious course. The Mediterranean had ceased to be a Roman lake. From one end of Europe to the other, the Christian states found themselves con fronted with the challenge of a new Oriental civilisation founded on a new Oriental faith." (H. A. L. Fisher, "A History of Europe", pp. 137|8.)

How did that stupendous miracle happen ? That has been one of the baffling questions for historians. To-day the educated world has rejected the vulgar theory that the rise of Islam was a triumph of fanaticism over sober and tolerant peoples. The phenomenal success of Islam was primarily due to its revolutionary significance and its ability to lead the masses out of the hopeless situation created by the decay of antique civilisations not only of Greece and Rome but of Persia and China—and of India.

CHAPTER TWO.

THE MISSION OF ISLAM.

VULGAR interpreters of the Islamic history lay stress upon its military achievements either to praise or to deprecate its far-reaching revolutionary significance. If the undoubtedly brilliant military conquests of the Saracens were the only measure of the historic role of Islam, then it would not be a unique historical phenomenon. The depradations of the barbarians of Tartary and Scythia (Goths, Huns, Vandals, Avars, Mongols etc.) approximated, if not equalled or excelled, their military accomplishments. But there is a vast difference between the tidal waves that occasionally rolled West, South and East, from the border land of Europe and Asia, and the Arabic eruption of religious frenzy. Like tidal waves the former rolled on in their cataclysmic greatness, only to subside, sooner or later, having distributed death and destruction, far and wide. The latter, on the contrary, was an abiding historical phenomenon, which ushered in a brilliant chapter of the cultural annals of mankind. Destruction was only a subsidiary part of its mission. It pulled down the played-out old, to construct a necessary new. It demolished the holy edifices of the Cesars and the Chosroes, only to rescue from their impending ruin the accumulated treasures of human knowledge, to preserve and multiply them for the benefit of the posterity.

The prodigious feats of the Saracen horsemen are not the only distinctive feature of Islam. They simply captivate our attention which must marvel at them, and impel us to search out and admire the causes of such a tremendously dynamic historical phenomenon. The miraculous performance of the "Army of God" usually dazzles the vision and the more magnificent achievements of the Islamic revolution are seldom known to the average student of history, even if he be a follower of Mohammad. Yet, the martial victories of the followers of the Arabian Prophet were but the prelude to a more magnificent and lasting performance in the social and cultural fields. They only created the conditions for political unity which opened up an era of economic prosperity and spiritual progress. The stupendous ruins of the Roman and Persian Empires had to be cleared away so that a new social order could rise with new ideas and new ideals. The dark superstition of the Magian mysticism, and the corrupt atmosphere of the Greek Church vitiated the spiritual life of the subjects of the decrepit Persian and Byzantine Empires rendering all moral and intellectual progress impossible. The severe monotheism of Mohammad wielded the formidable scimiter of the Saracen not only to destroy the profane idolatry of the Arabian tribes; it also proved to be the invincible instrument of history for freeing a considerable section of mankind from the eternal evil spirit of Zoroaster as well as from degenerate Christianity given to the superstition of miracle-mongering, to the deadly disease of monasticism and to the idolatrous worship of Saints. The amazing achievements of Saracen arms only prove that they were wielded at the service of history—for the progress of humanity.

The rich spiritual legacy of the glorious civilisation of ancient Greece was almost buried under the dreary ruins of the Roman Empire, and lost in the darkness of Christian superstition. The grand mission of rescuing the invaluable patrimony, which eventually enabled the peoples of Europe to emerge from the depressing gloom of the holy middle-ages, and build the marvellous monument of modern civilisation, belonged to the Saracen arms, and to the socio-political structure erected on the basis of Islamic Monotheism. The sword of Islam, wielded ostensibly at the service of God, actually contributed to the victory of a new social force—the blossoming of a new intellectual life—which eventually dug the grave of all religions and faiths.

Islam rose rather as a political movement than a religion in the strictest sense of the word. In the initial stages of its history, it was essentially a call for the unity of the nomadic tribes inhabiting the Arabian desert. Upon its speedy realisation, the politic-religious unitarian doctorine became the flag under which the Asiatic and African provinces of the Roman Empire survived the dissolution of the antique social order. The previous revolt had miscarried itself. Christianity had lost its original revolutionary fervour becoming, on the one hand, the ideology of social dissolution (Monasticism), and a prop for the decaying Empire, on the other. But the social crisis continued, aggravated by the degeneration of Christianity. The message of hope and salvation came from the Caravan traders of Arabia who had stood outside the corrupting atmosphere of the decomposed Roman world, and prospered by their advantageous position. The "Revolt of Islam" saved humanity.

A famous authority on Islamic history writes the following about the mission of Mohammad: "He found a whole nation in the full tide of rapid improvement, eagerly in search of knowledge and power. The excitement in the public mind of Arabia, which produced the mission of Mahamet, induced many other prophets to make their appearance during his life time." (Okley, "History of the Saracens.")

The people, for whom Islamic history is summarised in the exploits of fanatical hords, dramatically offering the dismayed world the choice between the Koran and the sword, with the blood-curdling cry of "Allah Akhbar", do not know, or conveniently overlook, that only the immediate successors of Mohammad occupied themselves solely with temporal and religious conquests; and even they were distinguished from the barbarian ravishers of humanity like Alaric, Attila, Genseric, Chengis or Tamerlane, by the nobility of character, purity of purpose and piety of spirit. Their devoutness might have been fortified by superstition, but was not stained by hypocracy. Their fanaticism was softened by generosity and sound common-sense. Their ambition was remarkably free from selfishness. Godliness, for them, was not a veil for greediness.

There are few figures in history more romantic, more devout, more sincere and more modest than the first "Commander of the Faithful"—Abu Bakr. His memorable injunction to the "Army of God" ran: "Be just; the unjust never prosper. Be valiant; die rather than yield. Be merciful; slay neither old men, nor women, nor children. Destroy neither fruit trees, nor grains, nor cattle. Keep your word even to your enemy. Molest not those men who live retired from the world." The irresistable march of the "Army of God" bears testimony to that this remarkable injunction was uttered sincerely by the venerable chief, and obeyed strictly by the devout followers.

Everywhere, the Saracen invaders were welcome as deliverers by peoples oppressed, tyrannised and tormented by Byzantine corruption, Persian despotism and Christian superstition. Fanatically faithful to the revolutionary teachings of the Prophet, and obediently acting according to the noble, wise and eminently practical injunctions of the Khalif, the Saracen invaders easily enlisted the sympathy and support of the peoples they conquered. No invader can establish an abiding domination over conquered peoples, except with their active support or tacit toleration.

The second Khalif, Omar, whose impetuous horsemen had pushed their victorious march through the Persian Empire, to the distant banks of the Oxus, on the one side, and were masters of the second metropolis of the Roman world—Alexandria—on the other, made his triumphal entry into Jerusalem on a camel which also carried the entire royal provision and equipage—a small tent of coarse hair, a bag of corn, a bag of dates, a wooden bowl, and a leathern flask of water. Gibbon offers the following account of the simplicity, devoutness, equity, and righteousness of the conquerors of Persia, Mesopotamia, Syria, Palestine and Egypt: "Wherever he halted, the company without distinction was invited to partake of his homely fare, and the repast was consecrated by the prayer and exhortation of the Commander of the Faithful. But in expedition or pilgrimage, his power was exercised in the administration of justice; he reformed the licentious polygamy, the polygamy of the Arabs; relieved the tributaries from extortion and cruelty; and chastised the luxury of the Saracens by dispoiling them of their rich silk, and dragging them on their face in dirt." ("Decline and Fall of the Roman Empire.")

Khaled, whom the Prophet called the "Sword of God," whose almost legendary valour had united Arabia, Mesopotamia and Syria under the banner of Islam, died in the possession only of his horse, his arms, and a single slave. The great hero is credited to have declared in his youth, "it is not the delicacies of Syria, or the fading delights of this world, that have prompted me to devote my life in the cause of religion, I only seek the favour of God, and his apostle". (Recorded by the historian Abul Feda.)

The valiant conqueror of Egypt, Omrou, was distinguished by a poetic genius in addition to martial valour. The following remarkable passage occurs in his report to Khalif Omar: "The crowds of husbandmen who blacken the land may be compared to a swarm of industrious ants; and their native indolence is quickened by the lash of the taskmaster. But the riches they extract are unequally shared between those who labour and those who possess." That was a view far in advance of time. The idea of social equity was unknown in all the lands of ancient civilisation. The toilers, either as slaves or as *Sudras*, were the object of legitimate contempt and exploitation. They were hardly considered as human beings. The economic principle, primitively formulated in the memorable injunction of the first Khalif, evolved out of the interest of the Arab traders, revolutionised the old social idea. A part of the wealth produced by the toiling masses, when left with themselves, becomes a powerful impetus to trade. In his administration of the conquered kingdom of the Pharaos and the Ptolemies, the Arab warrior sought with success to mend the glaring inequities that had offended his poetic vision. Egypt, robbed and dispoiled for centuries by the Greeks and the Romans, prospered under the Saracens.

There is no end of testimonies to prove that even in the predominently martial period of their history, the Saracens were far from being barbaric bands of fanatical marauders, spreading pillage and rapine, death and destruction in the name of religion. Then, the period of conquest was short, as compared to the long era of learning and culture that flourished subsequently under the patronage of the Khalifs as well as of the tributary and independent Empire. The military period terminated with the establishment of the Abbassides at Bagdad—the "City of Peace"—just about a hundred years after the ascendancy of the Prophet at Medina. Since then, the military activities of the Arabs were essentially of the nature of current defensive and offensive operations of a far-flung Empire.

The stern enthusiasm of the Saracen warriors was softened by time and prosperity. They began to seek riches no longer in war, but in trade and industry; fame, not on the field of battle, but in the pursuit of science and literature; and happiness, no longer in the fanatical worship of one God and his only Prophet, but in the harmless enjoyment of social and domestic life. War was no longer the passion and proud profession of the Saracens, because they had found interest and delight in a peaceful world created by the prowess of their forefathers. The progeny of the intrepid heroes, who had flocked to the belligerent standard of Abu Bakr and Omar, with the hope of paradise and incidentally earthly spoils, found the modest occupation of trade and industry more profitable, and science and philosophy more gratifying.

Three hundred years of peace, prosperity and progress elapsed before the martial valour of the Saracens was rekindled by

Christian aggression in the deceptive form of the crusades. Pillage and plunder, tyranny and oppression came to be associated with Muslim conquests only after the power of the Saracens had been overwhelmed by the Mongol barbarians from Central Asia; Arab learning and culture had been corrupted by the degenerating luxury of the court; and the proud standard of Islam, having lost its original revolutionary lustre, had been prostituted in the rapacious hands of the Turks and the Tartars.

It is a gross misreading of history to confound Islam with militarism. Mohammad was the Prophet not of the Saracen warriors, but of the Arab merchants. The very name with which he baptised his creed contradicts the current notion about its aim. Etymologically, Islam means to make peace, or the making of peace: to make peace with God by doing homage to his Oneness, repudiating the fraudulent divinity of idols which had usurped His sole claim to the devotion of man; and to make peace on earth through the union of the Arabian tribes. The peace on earth was of immediate importance, and greater consequence. The temporal interest of the Arabian merchants required it; for, trade thrives better under peaceful conditions. Since decayed states and degenerated religions bred the germs of continued wars and perennial revolts, their destruction was a condition for peace. The creed of Mohammad made peace at home, and the martial valour of the Saracans conferred the same blessing on the peoples inhabiting the vast territories from Samarcand to Spain.

As soon as a country came under the domination of the Arabs, its economic life was quickened by the encouragement of industry and agriculture. The spirit and interest of the Arab traders determined and directed the policy of the Islamic State. In the Roman world as well as in all the other lands of antique civilisation, the ruling classes detested all productive labour,—looked down upon trade and industry. War and worship were their noble professions. With the Arabs, it was different. Nomadic life in a desert had taught them to appreciate labour as the source of freedom. With them, trade was an honourable as well as a lucrative occupation of the free man. Thus, the Islamic State was based upon social relations entirely different from those of the old. Religion extolled industry, and encouraged a normal indulgence of nature. Trade was free, and as noble a profession as state craft war, letter and science. The

Khalifs of Bagdad were not only great traders; the earlier ones learned, and actually practiced some craft to purchase their personal necessities with the proceeds of manual labour. Most of the great Arab philosophers and scholars came from opulent trading families. The culture and refinement of the courts of Bokhara and Samarcand, the munificence of the Fatemite rulers of Africa and the splendour of the Sultans of Andalusia were equally produced rather by the profits of prosperous trade than by taxes exorted by despotic measures.

Under certain conditions, trade is a potent instrument of spiritual revolution. The aspiration of the Arab merchant produced the Monotheism of Mohammad. This, in its turn, inspired the nomads of a desert to establish one of the vastest and most flourishing empires of history. The laws of Koran revolutionised social relations. Increased production, the result of this revolution, quickened trade which ushered in an era of cosmopolitanism and spiritual uplift. Trade broadens the vision of man. Visiting distant lands, getting used to the sight of strange customs, mixing with peoples of diverse races, the trader frees himself from the prejudices and limitations born of the local conditions of his native land. He develops the capacities of toleration, sympathy and understanding for the habits, views and faiths of others. Observation and inquisitiveness, which guide his voyage on the unknown sea, or direct his steps in lands, kill in him the comfort of credulity. The growth of critical faculty places him at the gate of knowledge. The essense of his occupation teaches the trader to think in abstraction. He is not interested in his merchandise as such. His mind is occupied with the idea of profit. It is all the same to him whether his camels or ships are ladden with wool or corn or spices. He is concerned with something which is neither these nor other concrete things he handles. These are simply the means to attain his end—to make profit which is a category abstracted from the concrete commodity he buys or sells. He appreciates things, not in their intrinsic value, but according to their capacity to produce profit.

Toleration for strange things, the attempt to understand them, freedom from prejudice, faculty of observation, ability to think in abstract—all these qualities acquired by the trader, thanks to the nature of his occupation, go into the making of a philosophical outlook. Having seen different peoples cherish diverse forms of superstitions as divine wisdom, practise equally absurd rites and rituals or expressing devotion, extol prejudices to the dignity of eternal truth, the cosmopolitan mind of the travelled trader indulgently smiles upon the credulity of all, deplores their depravity equally, and respects the common element of faith beneath the superficial diversities of theological dogmas and forms of worship.

The main arteries of international trade of the mediæval world ran through the countries which embraced Islam and were united in the Saracen Empire. The northern routes of trade with China, which passed through Constantinople to Italy and other countries of Western Europe, had become extremely risky owing to the Scythian inroads and the ruinous fiscal policy of the Byzantine Empire. After their conquest of Syria, Mesopotamia, Persia and the territories across the Oxus, the Arabs captured the Chinese trade and diverted it to pass through their domain of North-Africa and Spain, ultimately to reach the markets of Western Europe. During the eighth to the eleventh centuries, practically the entire trade between India and China, on the one hand, and Europe, on the other, was done by the Arabs. Thousands of traders travelled with their Caravans, loaded with precious cargoes, from the remote frontiers of China and India all the way to Morocco and Spain. They were not persecuted or detested as their kind had been in all the countries of antique civilisation with the honourable exception of Greece. In the Empire of the Saracens, they belonged to the ruling class. Consequently, the learning and culture, that thrived so luxuriantly owing to the prosperity of the Saracen Empire, bore the stamp of their native broad-mindedness, cosmopolitanism and incredulity. Under the leadership of a martial aristocracy and jealous priesthood, human ideology takes the form of dogmatic faith for misty mysticism. Philosophy—the search for a rational explanation of the Universe originates in a society ruled by an aristocracy engaged in trade. The city states of the Ionian Greeks were therefore the birthplaces of philosophy.

Islam was a necessary product of history, —an instrument of human progress. It rose as the ideology of a new social relation which, in its turn, revolutionised the mind of man. But just as it had subverted and replaced older cultures, decayed in course of time, Islam, in its turn, was also overstepped by further social developments, and consequently had to hand over its spiritual leadership to other agencies born out of newer conditions. But it contributed to the forging of new ideological instruments which brought about the subsequent social revolution. The instruments were experimental science and rationalist philosophy. It stands to the credit of Islamic culture to have been instrumental in the promotion of the ideology of a new social revolution.

Capitalist mode of production rescued Europe from the chaos of mediæval barbarism. It fought and in the long run vanquished Christian theology and the spiritual monopoly of the Catholic Church with the potent weapon of rationalist philosophy. This weapon, invented by the ancient sages of Greece came to the possession of the founders of modern civilisation through the Arab scholars who had not only preserved the precious patrimony, but added to it handsomely. The historic battle, begun by the nomads of the Arabian desert, under the religious flag of Islam, was fought step by step through a thousand years on fields scattered over the three continents, to be won finally in Europe under the profane standard of the eighteenth century Enlightenment and Bourgeois Revolution.

CHAPTER THREE.

SOCIAL AND HISTORICAL BACKGROUND OF ISLAM.

ISLAM—the Religion of Peace—was not the creation of Mohammad any more than other religions were of those to whom their origins are respectively attributed. No religion is the creation of any single individual, nor does it appear all of a sudden, revealed to this or that Seer as it is always claimed. Islam, like any other religion, was the product of the conditions of the time, and of the surroundings in which it flourished.)

Though living on the side of the fateful road, on which the conquering armies of the Assyrians, Persians, Macedonians and Romans had marched back and forth, the inhabitants of the vast Arabian Peninsula maintained their freedom by virtue of the natural aspects of their country and the mode of life moulded by those aspects. But the fierce love of freedom, together with the exigencies of a nomadic existence, had split the inhabitants of the Arabian desert into a number of tribes perpetually engaged in feuds and warfare.

Separated from the rest of mankind, the Arabs took the stranger for an enemy. The poverty of his country had added to the growth of that spirit. These two factors went into the making of the codes of law and morality of the Arabs. They believed that, as descendants of the outlawed Ismael, they were doomed to live in a dreary desert while rich and fertile lands were assigned to the other branches of the human family. Consequently, they felt themselves justified in recovering by force a portion of the heritage, they believed, they had been deprived of.

The Roman historian Pliny, six hundred years before the appearance of Mohammad, found the Arabs occupied with two lucrative professions, robbery and trade, in addition to their native call of sheep-raising and horse-breeding. In the earlier stages of social evolution, these two professions of robbery and trade are usually distinguished by a thin and elastic line of demarcation. The trader makes his profit by purchasing things at the cheapest price, and selling them at the highest. The cheaper the price he pays, the greater is his profit. Robbery or theft places him in possession of things at the lowest price. Therefore, once the morality of the fundamental principle of trading is admitted, the right of the trader to act so as to make the greatest possible profit becomes legitimate. Then, competition keeps the price of his wares down. The most convenient way of eliminating competition is to rob the rival. By that stratagem, not only is the competitor kept away from the market, but his goods go there as the property of the more efficient party. Further, robbery is an effective weapon to establish monopoly on trade-routes and markets. In its earlier stages of development, trade is everywhere conducted with these practical policies which must shock a modern merchant. Still, robbery was the weapon with which his less orthodox predecessors established the noble profession which he now carries on so righteously with the laudable maxim: Honesty is the best policy.

Besides, robbery imperceptibly ripens into the manly political virtue of warlikeness, so much glorified in the savage adolescence of mankind. Given to robbery by the physical aspects of their homeland, the Arabs were naturally destined to develop unusual talent in trade as well as in war. Their bravery and warlikeness were almost legendary. The famous historical work. "Ayam al Arab," composed in the most flourishing days of the Saracen Empire, records no less than seventeen hundred memorable battles fought by the Arabs before the rise of the Prophet. So, if the Saracens distinguish themselves as warriors, they did not derive that virtue from their Islamic faith. They had been warriors before they were called to wield the sword in the service of God. The military achievements of Islam should be credited not so much to the religious teachings of the Arabic Prophet as to the social conditions of the country in which it was born.

The wars conducted by the Arabs before the appearance of the Prophet were mostly internecine feuds, fought with savage fierceness, but strictly according to the quaint codes of honour, chivalry and nobility. The profuse spilling of blood did not fertilise the sands of Arabia, but it did, eventually, become prejudicial to the profitable economic consequences of robbery, the legitimate profession of trade conducted by the primitive Arabs. Economic necessity demanded termination of the proud but ruinous virtue of internecine wars, and diversion of the traditional Saracen valour in more profitable channels. The ideas, born out of that necessity, eventually crystallised into the "Religion of Mohammad."

Itself a vast stretch of sandy wilderness, Arabia, however, is surrounded on three sides by fruitful, populous countries-homes of ancient civilisations, where industry and agriculture thrived from time immemorial. On the south is the ocean on which navigated vessels carrying the trade of India. Thanks to her geographical position, Arabia was interested by the routes of Caravan trade and maritime commerce, interchanged among India, Persia, Assyria, Syria, Palestine, Egypt and Abyssinia. In earlier days, the trade-routes connecting Africa and Asia lay through the south and north of the Peninsula, avoiding the unknown interior of the sandy wilderness. But the exorbitant taxation of Byzantine despotism, supplemented by the endless extortion of its local officials, drove the traders to hazard the encounter of the fierce, but hospitable Beduin in the heart of his home.

In the beginning, the Arab collected his tribute according to his peculiar code of law and morality. But in course of time, he discovered that trade would be more profitable than robbery. Of all the Arabian tribes, the Koreish were the first to exchange the turbulent for a peaceful, but more profitable profession. They inhabited the coast-line of the Red Sea, and had commanded the Abyssinian trade long before the Asiatic traffic also came their way. In the earlier centuries of the Christian era, the capital of the Koreish tribe, Mecca, had become the point where the important trade-routes from south to north and east to west intersected. At Yamen, on the Arabian Sea, the Koreish caravans took over the commodities from India; at a point near modern Aden, their precious burden was increased by the African riches from Abyssinia. The journey northwards terminated at the busy marts of Damascus, where corn and manufactured articles were bought at the exchange of aromatics, pearls, precious stones, tusks etc. The lucrative exchange diffused plenty and riches in the streets of Macca. When, later, the east-west trade-route also passed through Mecca, the prosperity of the Koreish became unbounded, and their ambition proportionately grew.

But other Arabian tribes, jealous of their freedom, and envious of the prosperity of the Koreish, stood faithfully by their traditional codes of law and morality, whose profane origin was no longer admitted. They were raised to the nobility of offensive and defensive warfare, on the authority of tribal gods. The old national pastime of robbery which had previously been played at the expense of unwary strangers, turned out ruinous to the new national occupation of trade. Termination of the tribal feuds became an essential condition for further political task of establishing unity, by the logic of historical events, devolved upon those who controlled the economic forces making for the historically necessary goal. The Koreish appeared as the chosen people of history.

In the midst of their ceaseless feuds, all the Arabian tribes worshipped and sacrificed at the temple of Caabba near Mecca. The Koreish had seized the control of the seat of national worship, and the sacredotal office of great power and extensive privilege had been captured by the Hashemites—the most important family of the tribe. The Hashemites, therefore, commanded national respect and veneration, in addition to the opulence derived from trade. Eventually, a scion of the Hashemite family issued the call for unity in the form of a new religion which denied all gods but one.

The severe Monotheism of Mohammad not only echoed the yarning for unity on the part of a people torn assunder by internecine feuds; it was also destined to find a ready response from the neighbouring nations, tormented by the intolerance of the Catholic Church. The religious life of the people of Persia, Mesopotamia, Syria, Palestine and Egypt had been hopelessly confused by the conflicts of Magian Mysticism, Jewish conservatism and Christian bigotry. Rigid rites and rituals had taken the place of religion; hypocritical ceremonies had driven away devotion; dogmatic theology had prosecuted faith; and God had disappeared in a confusing crowd of angels, saints and apostles. The stringent cry of the new religion.—"There is but One God"—softened by great toleration, subject to this fundamental creed, was enthusiastically hailed by the distressed multitudes searching for the secure anchor of a simple faith in the stormy sea of social disintegration, intellectual bankruptcy and spiritual chaos. The historic cry was raised by the caravan traders of Arabia who had stood outside the ruinous conflict of arms and beliefs, had prospered economically, and progressed in spirit, while their older and more civilised neighbours had stagnated, decayed and disintegrated. The propagation of the stern belief in the Oneness of God prepared the ground for the rise of a military State which unified all the social functions—religious, civil, judicial and administrative. The unitarianism of the Saracens layed the foundation of a new social order which rose magnificently out of the ruins of the antique civilisation. Such a creed was sure to attract the attention of the multitudes barbarously persecuted for religious heterodoxy. The new faith allowed freedom of conscience to all who placed themselves under its protection. Islam rose as a protection against religious persecution and refuge for the oppressed

The accomodating nature, cosmopolitan spirit, democratic policy and the monotheistic creed of Islam were the creation of the geographical position of the land of its birth. Surrounded with countries oppressed by native despotism or devastated by foreign invasions, Arabia maintained her freedom. The persecuted sects from Egypt and Persia as well as from the Christiandom fled to the free and hospitable desert where they could profess what they thought, and practice what they professed. When the

Empire of the Assyrians was conquered by the Persians, and the altars of Babylon subverted by the Magis, the Sabian priests retired to the neighbouring desert with their ancient faith and the precious knowledge of astronomy. Previously, Assyrian invasion had driven many a devout son of Isræl in the same hospitable wilderness. All the Hebrœ prophets, down to John the Baptist, lived, meditated and preached in the depth of the Arabian desert. The invasion of Alexander having avenged the wrong done to the Assyrians, the more orthodox disciples of Zoroaster, who did not wish to desecrate the purity of their faith by the toleration of Greek idolatry, migrated to the free atmosphere of the Arabian desert to join their hands with Babylonian adversaries.

Gnosticism and Manichæism—those hybrids of oriental mystic cults—Greek metaphysics and Christian Gospel, all thrived luxuriantly on the sandy soil of free Arabia. Finally, Catholic orthodoxy drove to the same smelting pot of Arabian hospitality the Nestorian, Jacobite and Eutycian heretics who preferred the simplicity of the Gospel to the idolatry of the orthodox Church. The freedom of exile brought the representatives of those diverse faiths into closer contact enabling them to see what was common to them all. In the calm atmosphere of toleration, their heterodoxy disappeared, fire of proselytism died out, and the common essence of the teachings of the learned guests was imparted to the hospitable Beduin. In short, the Barbarians of the desert inherited the best the religions of antiquity had to offer, namely, the faith in the existence of one supreme God who is exalted above all the powers of heaven and earth, but who had revealed himself to the mankind from time to time through his Prophets. Here is the essence of Islam crystallised in the spiritual consciousness of the Arabian people before Mohammad appeared with the mission of building a new religion on its basis. The spirit of Islam was not invented by the genius of Mohammad; nor was it revealed to him. It was a heritage of history conferred on the Arabian nation. The greatness of Mohammad was his ability to recognise the value of the heritage and make his countrymen conscious of it.

The Arabs had acquired the notion of one supreme God; but out of habit and for tribal interests, they still practised their old polytheistic worship. To be benefitted by the positive outcome of earlier religions, delivered to them as a heritage of history, they must change their traditional mode of worship. A supreme effort must be made with the purpose; and Mecca was the most strategic point to lead the attack from.

The particularist freedom and internecine feuds of the Arabian tribes were mutually compromised and composed at Mecca. All routes of trade led there. The unity of the economic interest of the decentralised nation had created at Mecca a symbol of precarious spiritual unity. All the tribes from distant parts of the vast desert, while visiting the market of Cecca, worshipped in the temple of Caabba. Each had introduced there its own emblem of devotion. The temple had been adorned with no less than three hundred and sixty idols of men, eagles, lions, etc., But the prosperous tribe of Koreish dominated the trade of Mecca, and the powerful family of Hashim had seized control of the temple. It was natural that the new spirit of a rising faith, which would further economic interest through national unity, should be first felt consciously at the heart of the nation. So, it happened that a member of the Hashimite family began to preach the new religion.

Once the family of Hashim and the tribe of Koreish were converted to the new faith, the whole nation would follow soon.

All the tribes must visit Mecca for the purposes of trade. Those who controlled the trade of Mecca could easily dictate the faith and conscience of the entire nation. But prejudice and habit induced the Koreish to persecute ennovating zeal of their kinsman. They were afraid that trade would be driven away from Mecca, should the Pantheon of Caabba be disturbed. But there were others ready to assume the leadership of the revolution, when the most eligible candidate failed. Medina espoused the cause of the Prophet, and the call of unity found enthusiastic response in other quarters. The supremacy of Mecca was menaced. One family after another defected from the Koreish conservatism, and joined the revolutionary Hashemites. Before long, the Koreish capitulated before their exiled kinsmen, but only to capture the sceptre of the "Commander of the Faithful."

As soon as the followers of the Prophet captured Mecca, a perpetual law was passed that no unbeliever should be allowed to set foot on the territory of the Holy City. The new religion was imposed upon the entire nation with the potent weapon of economic boycott. Caabba was cleared of its idols, and became the shrine of "Mohammad's God." Once the standard of the new religion was raised, the whole nation flocked under it. The ground had been prepared. The faith had unconsciously taken hold of the mind of the nation before it was preached. Economic interest demanded its establishment.

CHAPTER FOUR.

THE CAUSES OF TRIUMPH.

ITS historical background and the social conditions in which it was born put on Islam the stamp of toleration, which, to the undescerning eye, may appear to be incongruous with the spirit of fanaticism traditionally associated with it. But there is no contradiction. The basic doctrine of Islam—"There is but One God"—itself makes for toleration. If the whole world, with its defects and deformities, the entire mankind, with all its follies and frivolities, is admitted as the creation of the selfsame God, the believer in this elevating doctrine may deplore the deformities and laugh at what appears to him to be absurdities and perverseness; but the very nature of his faith does not permit him to look upon them as the works or worships of some other God of Evil, and declare war upon them as such.

Those, who worship differently, are for him mistaken and misled brethren, but none the less children of the selfsame Father, to be brought to the right road, or indulgently tolerated until they are ready for redemption.

The terrifying vision of the followers of the Arabic Prophet offering to the world, Koran or the sword, cast such an ominous shadow over the history of the rise of Islam as concealed the third alternative so freely offered, and generally accepted. That was the main cause for the triumph of Islam. As a matter of fact, the alternatives were very differently offered. It was: "Accept the Koran or pay tribute to the Saracen conqueror!" The "Sword of God" was unsheathed only when neither of the alternatives was accepted. The economic interest of the Arab trader, which produced the monotheistic creed of Islam, was antagonistic to indiscriminate bloodshed. The lands through which the trade-routes lay must be conquered and brought under the domination of the unitary State. The object would be all the better realised, should the conquered peoples accept the new religion; for, then the unitarian State would be established on a solid foundation. But production and consumption of commodities are the essential factors of trade. Therefore, it was not compatible with the historic role of Islam to massacre the artisan and peasant masses, or to destroy opulent cities for the impiety of. rejecting the Koran. What was necessary was their subjugation to the believers of the new creed. Under the domination of the followers of the Prophet, unbelieving peoples were allowed to hold their imperfect faiths, and to continue their perverse worships.

When Jerusalem capitulated to Khalif Omar, the inhabitants of the vanquished city were left in possession of their worldly goods, and allowed the freedom of worship A special quarter of the city was allotted for the residence of the Christian population with their Patriarch and his clergy. For the protection thus granted, a nominal tax of two pieces of gold was imposed upon the entire Christian community. The pilgrimage to the Holy City was stimulated rather than suppressed by the Muslim conquerors, on account of the commercial value of that devout traffic. Four hundred and sixty years later, when the Holy Land reverted to the Christian rule of the crusading knights of Europe, "the Oriental Christians regretted the tolerating Government of the Arabian Khalifs". (Gibbon, "Rise and Fall of the Roman Empire".)

In contrast to the toleration of the Muslims, the following account of the occupation of Jerusalem by the Crusaders is highly illuminating: "In the pillage of private and public wealth, the adventurers had agreed to respect the exclusive property of the first occupant. A bloody sacrifice was offered by mistaken votaries to the God of the Christians; resistance might provoke, but neither sage nor sex could mollify, their implacable rage; they indulged themselves three days in a promiscuous massacre. After seventy thousand Muslims had been put to the sword, and the harmless Jews had been burned in their Synagogue, they could still reserve a multitude of captives whom interest or lassitude persuaded them to spare." (Ibid).

On the testimony of a whole series of authoritative historians, Christian as well as Muslim, contemporary as well as modern, the critical Gibbon conclusively proves that "to his Christian subjects, Mohammad readily granted security of their persons, the freedom of their trade, the property of their goods and the toleration of their worship." This profitable principle of toleration was observed with more or less strictness, not only by all the immediate successors of the Prophet, but over the whole period of Arabic ascendency. It was abandoned only after Islam had played out its historic role, and its leadership has passed from the noble Saracens to the notorious barbariahs of Tartary. Even under the first Turkish Sultans, Islam was not completely divorced from its original spirit of toleration.

In its days of glory, the native toleration of Islam not only developed into wide freedom of thought and rationalism, but, from the orthodox point of view, even degenerated into positively heretical and irreligious notions. Most of the earlier Abbassides Khalifs of Bagdad were not only devoted to the study of profane science, and free in their thought; some of them, Motassen for example, even did not believe in the divine origin of the Koran.

For centuries, the Saracen Empire offered hospitable asylum to the persecuted Jews as well as to the unorthodox Christians sects of the Nestorians, Jacobites, Eutychians and Paulicians. After the consolidation of the Saracen conquest, the toleration of Islam was extended even to the Catholic Church. Many Christian historians themselves bear testimony to this effect. The Ecclesiastical historian Renaudot, for example, informs that "the rank, the immunities, and the domestic jurisdiction of Patriarchs, Bishops, and the clergy were protected by the (Muslim) civil magistrates (of Egypt); the leaning of Christian individuals recommended them to the employment of secretaries and physicians; they were enriched by the lucrative collection of revenue; and their merit was sometimes raised to the command of cities and provinces." A Khalif of Bagdad declared that the Christians were most worthy of trust in the administration of Persia. The Paulicians, those valiant fore-runners of the Protestant Reformation, not only received freedom of worship in the Saracen Empire, but were actively supported by the Khalifs in their prolonged effort to subvert the degenerated Catholic Church, and re-establish Christianity in its original form.

The ancient religion of Zoroaster, with its pernicious doctrine of the dual principles of Good and Evil, both equally eternal, was particularly obnoxious to the stern worshipper of "One God". Yet, even the Magian creed did not altogether forfeit the toleration of the conquering Arab. As late as the third century of the Hegira, ancient temples of Fire stood splendourously overshadowing the modest Mosque by their side. Those proud monuments of an ancient faith crumbled not under the ruthless blow of the fanatical Sword of Islam; they were doomed to destruction, and fall to inevitable ruins in consequence of the general desertion of their votaries. No amount of coercion could possibly force a whole nation to abandon its traditional faith with so little resistance, and accept that of the conqueror with such surprising alacrity, as did the Persians over the vast territory from the Tigris to the Oxus. The ancient faith was decayed. It no longer satisfied the spiritual requirements of a cultured people. The menacing shadow of Khariman had eclipsed the lustre of the "Sun and Fire." The Persian masses embraced the simple Monotheism of Mohammad as the message of liberation from the dark despotism of the eternal principle of Evil.

The north of Africa, from Alexandria to Carthage, was the only territory where the Christian faith was totally obliterated by the spread of Islam. There again, the cause of the sweeping religious revolution was not the intolerance of the new creed, but the decay of the old faith, and the general chaos and despair caused by that decay. The faith of the gospel of Jesus, established by the talent, piety and power of Cyprian, Athanasius and Augustin, had been subverted by Arian and Donatist heresies, and the Catholic fury, with which the improverished masses revolting under the banner of religious heresy were suppressed, had ruined the once prosperous provinces economically. Then, the Vandal and Moorish invader had devastated the ruins so mercilessly as to throw the people into a hopeless state of social chaos and spiritual morbidity which drove them to seek an illusive solace in the absurdities of Monasticism.

In that dense darkness of social dissolution and spiritual despair, the virile and opitimistic message of the Prophet of Arabia flashed like an illuminating flame of hope. The mind of the multitude was lured by the temporal as well as the heavenly blessings offered by the new religion. The conquering trumpet of Islam awakened the despondent spirits who, defeated in the struggle of terrestrial life, had precariously entrenched themselves in the superstition of a divine existence. Healthy indulgence of nature, allowed, even encouraged, by the new faith, speedily overwhelmed the perverse notions of asceticism fomented by a degenerate version of the gospel of Christ. Islam opened up a new vision of hope before a people, sunk in the depth of despondency.

The convulsion created by it ushered in a new society in which every one had the opportunity of ascending the natural level of his courage and capacity. With the exhilarating inspiration of Islam, and under the benevolent rule of the Saracen conquerors, the fertile soil and industrious peoples of North Africa soon recovered fruitfulness and prosperity.

"It is altogether a misconception that the Arabian progress was due to the sword alone. The sword may change an acknowledged national creed, but it cannot affect the consciences of men. Profound though its argument is, something far more profound was demanded before Mohammadanism pervading the domestic life of Asia and Africa.......The explanation of this political phenomenon is to be found in the social condition of the conquered countries. The influences of religion in them had long ago ceased; it had become supplanted by theology....... How was it possible that unlettered men, who with difficulty can be made to apprehend obvious things, should understand such mysteries? Yet, they were taught that on those doctrines the salvation or damnation of the human race depended. They saw......that personal virtue or vice were no longer considered; that sin was not measured by evil works but by the degrees of heresy.......What an example when bishops are concerned in assassinations, poisonings, adulteries, blindings, riots, treasons, civil war; when Patriarchs and Primats were excommunicating and anathematising one another in their rivalries for earthly power, bribing Eunuchs with gold, and courtesans and royal females with concessions of episcopal love, and influencing the decisions of councils asserted to speak with the voice of God by those base intrigues and sharp practices resorted to by demagogues in their packed assemblies! Among legions of monks, who carried terror into the imperial armies and riot into the great cities, arose hideous clamours for theological dogmas, but never a voice for intellectual liberty or the outraged rights of man. In such a state of things, what else could be the result than disgust or indifference? Certainly men could not be expected......to give help to a system that had lost all hold on their hearts.

"When, therefore, in the midst of the wrangling of sects......and anarchy of countless disputants, there sounded through the world......the dread battle cry, 'There is but One God',......is it surprising that the hubbub was hushed ? Is it surprising that all Asia and Africa fell away? In better times, patriotism is too often made subordinate to religion; in those times, it was altogether dead." (J. W. Draper, "History of the Intellectual Development of Europe", Vol. I, pp. 332|3.)

The principle of equality, preached by the followers of Mohammad, originated in the traditional freedom of the nomadic life of the Arabic tribes. They had all shown equal valour in the national profession of robbery. When that modest call of the olden times assumed the majestic proportion of conquest, the individual Arab did not forget that his horse could speed as fast and his scimitar was as sharp as those of any. He had taken an equal share in defending his desert home against the conquering armies of Sesostris and Cyrus, Alexander and Darius, Pompei and Ashirwan, Ptolemy and Trajan. He would not play a less noble part in the pastime of turning the table. But the principle of equality proclaimed by Islam proved to be a factor in its spectacular triumph no less potent than the scimitar of the Saracen hero. It contrasted sharply with the oppressive laws governing the class and caste-ridden societies of the Roman Byzantine, Persian and, later, of Indian Empires. Islam stood for freedom and equality which, as a matter of fact, had long been forgotten in all the lands of the degenerated ancient civilisation.

The proud possession of the spiritual heritage of earlier civilisations having accrued to the Arabs, it became their mission to share it with the unfortunate multitudes groaning under the hideous ruins of those civilisations. The circumstances of the age were favourable to the dramatic expansion of Islam. It rose in the period of intellectual and spiritual decline of the ruling classes throughout the world of ancient civilisations. The dissatisfaction with the social conditions of decay, decomposition, and despotism had created in the masses of people the aspiration and striving for a better world. Christianity had been the first child born of that revolutionary spirit. The unfortunate triumph of having enlisted the currupting patronage of the old ruling class had transformed Christianity into an apologist of the established order of society. The Church Fathers had conveniently forgotten that their Prophet preached revolt against the Roman yoke, and had painted him as the meek sheep bleating the shameful injunction: "Pay the Caesar his due"—an injunction which violated the whole tradition of Jewish history constituting the background of Christianity. Having compromised with the ruling class, Christianity could not but betray the mission of laying the foundation of a new social order commensurate with the objective striving of the age. It had refused to lead the destitute to the conquest of this world and had deceived them with the delusion of a world to come, flowing with milk and honey. The entrance to the Kingdom of Heaven was to be allowed only to the meek, that is, to those who would submit to the tyranny of the rulers of this world.

The debacle of Christianity made the appearance of a more vigorous religion an historical necessity. Islam not only promised its votaries the blessings of a brilliant paradise. It also inspired them to the conquest of this world. Indeed, the Paradise of the Arabian Prophet was nothing but an ideal of the life of happiness and enjoyment to be attained in this world. Mohammad not only provided his own people with a platform of national unity, but armed the united Arabian nation with a cry of revolt which found ready response from the oppressed and destitute masses in all the adjacent countries.

The cause of the dramatic success of Islam was spiritual as well as social and political. On this important point, Gibbon testifies: "More pure than the system of Zoroaster, more liberal than the laws of Moses, the religion of Mohammad might seem less inconsistent with reason than the creed of mystery and superstition which, in the seventh century, disgraced the simplicity of the Gospel." ("Decline and Fall of the Roman Empire.")

Still one more historian bears testimony to the fact that the spectacular thriumph of Islam was rather due to its liberating and equalitarian principles than to the military valour of its early adherents. "In almost every case in which the Saracens conquered a Christian nation, history unfortunately reveals that they owed their success chiefly to the favour with which this progress was regarded by the masses of the conquered people. To the disgrace of most Christian governments, it will be found that their administration was more oppressive than that of the Arab conquerors.....The inhabitants of Syria welcomed the followers of Mahomet; the Copts of Egypt contributed to place their country under the domination of the Arabs; and the Christian Berbers aided the conquest of Africa. All these nations were induced, by the hatred for the government of Constantinople, to place themselves under the sway of the Mohammadans. The treachery of the nobles and the indifference of the people made Spain and the South of France easy prey to the Saracens." (Finlay, "History of the Byzantine Empire.")

CHAPTER FIVE.

MOHAMMAD AND HIS TEACHINGS.

THE founder of Islam has been characterised as "the man who, of all men, has exercised the greatest influence upon the human race." (Draper, "History of the Intellectual Development of Europe," Vol. I, p. 329). There was, however, nothing very extraordinary about the man until he claimed the credit of divine revelation. The foundation of that dubious claim was no more or no less fictitious than in the case of the prophets, apostles and saints of all other religions. Christian arrogance called the Arabian Prophet an "Imposter". But it has been forgotten that he was given that name together with Moses and Jesus. The authorship of the famous book, anonymously published,—"Three Imposters"—which created sensation in Europe towards the close of the middle-ages, was attributed to the

Christian King Frederic Barbarossa as well as to the Muslim philosopher Averroes.

If Mohammad was an "imposter", he did not take up that role any more consciously than others who appeared as instruments through which the fiction of divine revelation became a reality and carried conviction with the ignorant and superstitious masses. Having conceived the ideal of national unity, Mohammad realised that it could not be made acceptable to the warring Arabian tribes unless it were backed up with a supernatural sanction. People enjoying the bliss of ignorance and thinking in terms of preconceived notions, could not be convinced with any other argument. The will of minor gods could be overwhelmed by the will of a greater and all-powerful God. The protection against the wrath of the former should be found in the mercy of the latter. The belief in the absolute sway of one supreme God can alone encourage people to revolt against the tyranny of a whole host of tribal deities. If the supreme God was not there he had to be invented. That was the chain of Mohammad's thoughts. There was no imposture in it. Did not the rationalist Voltaire put forward the same argument more than a thousand years after it had found favour with the Arabian Prophet?

But in the latter case, the argument was put forward in defence of reaction; Voltaire advocated the necessity of inventing a God because that would be the only guarantee for the preservation of the decayed system of feudal monarchistic society. At the time of Mohammad, and under the circumstances it was advanced, the argument served a positively revolutionary purpose. When man's mind is dominated by the belief in the supernatural, every progressive idea should be formulated in the terms of those beliefs if it were to secure popular support. Besides, the idea of One God was not the invention of Mohammad. The idea had grown out of social conditions described in the last chapter. Mohammad's mission was to discover evidence for the existence of the One God. And if you wish to convince people you must adduce only that kind of evidence which can carry conviction to them.

But Mohammad's search for God was not inspired by cynicism as in the case of Voltaire. It was an honest effort on the part of an ignorant man inspired by a zeal. In quest of the God who alone could save the Arabian nation, he retired to the desert and gave himself up to meditation, fasting and prayer—those familiar practices adopted by the prejudiced seeking divine inspiration even in these days of the twentieth century. And the result was as usual in all such cases. "He was visited by supernatural appearances, mysterious voices accosted him as the Prophet of God; even the stones and trees joined in the whispering." (Draper Ibid.) Such experiences always result from cerebral disorder which takes place whenever the prescribed practices are carried too far. Fixed ideas, however fantastic or imaginary, may appear to take concrete form if the mind is focussed on them so as to exclude the consciousness of other sensations. A scientific study of the psychology of Seers reveals the fact that "inspiration" or any other "religious experience" is the result of a pathological state brought about either accidentally or purposely through prescribed practices.

Mohammad acted as all those of his kind had done before him, or did after him. But in his case, there was a fact which must go to his credit. He was too shrewd a man to be deluded by those psycho-pathological symptoms which are taken for the evidence of spiritual elevation. He was afraid that he was going mad; and might have abandoned his mission if his sagacious wife had not come to his aid in the nick of time. It was the rich merchant Khadija, mature with worldly wisdom, who was quick to appreciate the spiritual value of the mental aberrations of her husband. She persuaded him that his visions were not signs of insanity, but were messengers of God. Taking advantage of his psycho-pathological state of suggestibility, she could easily make him "see" an angel entering the room to deliver to him the Message of God. Undoubtedly, the drama could be enacted only in the setting of ignorance, superstition and prejudice, main characters being played under delusion. But that is how all religions are born. There is no reason to think that Islam was an exception. It was an exception in the sense that, except for the invention of a divine sanction, it contained less of religious dogmas and metaphysical speculation than sound political sense, progressive social principles and admirable codes of personal behaviour. "He did not engage in vain metaphysics, but applied himself to improving the social condition of his people by regulations respecting personal cleanliness, sobriety, fasting, prayer. Above all other works he esteemed almsgiving and charity. With a liberality to which the world had of late become a stranger, he admitted the salvation of men of any form of faith provided they were virtuous." (Draper, ibid.)

Composed by man of practically no education, the Koran, naturally, is not a work of any intellectual standard. It is full of crude ideas and phantastic speculations. These obvious defects of the Koran, easily over-shadow its great merit even as the source of inspiration of a great religion. Mohammad's religion was rigorously monotheistic; and as a Monotheism it was uncompromising, which outstanding characteristic won for it the distinction of the highest form of religion. The idea of God is the foundation of religion in the philosophical sense. That idea cannot be free of all fallacies unless it leads to the conception of creation out of nothing. The rationalism of ancient philosophers— of Greece as well as of India—excluded the fantastic conception. Consequently, religions growing out of the background of that primitive rationalism could not conclusively establish the fundamental idea of God. The result was that all the great religions—Hinduism, Judaism and Christianity—eventually ended in some or other form of pantheism which logically liquidates religion as such. For pantheism identiying the phenomenal world with God puts the very idea of God under doubt. It disposes of the idea of creation and, consequently, the idea of God must also go. If the world can exist, *by itself,* from eternity, it is not necessary to assume a creator. And, deprived of the function of creation, God becomes an unnecessary postulate.

Mohammad's religion cuts the Gordian knot. It frees the idea of God from the embarrassment of primitive rationalism by boldly asserting the highly irrational idea of creation out of nothing. The God stands out in all His glory. The ability to create not only the whole world but an endless series of worlds is the token of His all-powerfulness. To have thus established the idea of God, albeit in a dogmatic and primitive manner, was the credit of Mohammad. For that credit he has gone down in history as the founder of the purest form of religion. Because Islam as a religion is irrationalism *par excellence,* it so easily triumphed over all other religions which, with all their metaphysical accomplishments, theological subtleties and philosophical pretensions, were defective as religion, being but pseudo-religions.

Monotheism, however, is a highly subversive theory. While being itself the highest form of religion, it strikes at the root the religious mode of thought. Placing God above and beyond the world, it opens up the possibility of doing without him altogether. Islam as the most rigorous monotheistic religion closed the chapter of human history dominated by the religious mode of thought, and by its very nature was open to unorthodox interpretations which eventually liquidated the religious mode of thought and laid down the foundation of modern rationalism. "We may compare the working of Monotheism to a mighty lake, which gathers the floods of science together, until they suddenly begin to break through the dam........ The third of the great monotheistic religions, Mohammadanism, is more favourable to Materialism. This, the youngest of them, was also the first to develop, in connection with the brilliant outburst of Arabian civilisation, a free philosophical spirit, which exercised a powerful influence primarily upon the Jews in the middle ages, and so indirectly upon the Christians of the West." (F.A. Lange "The History of Materialism," Vol. I, pp. 174 and 177). Being the most perfected form of Monotheism, Islam played that role. The crudities of the Koran did not prevent its basic idea from flourishing into all its revolutionary consequences.

His severe Monotheism contradicted Mohammad's claim to the sole Prophecy of

God. While the Koran recognised Moses, Jesus and other Hebrew Prophets as apostles of God, Mohammad's claim, if not openly disputed in the beginning, was secretly doubted even among his associates. Divinity of its founder is not the fundamental creed of Islam. And that distinction results from its strict Monotheism. Immediately upon the death of Mohammad, his followers were divided on that crucial question. When the news of the Prophet's death reached the camp of the army setting out for the conquest of Syria, the devout Omar refused to believe that the Prophet could die, and threatened to strike off the head of messenger whom he suspected to be an infidel. Upon that, the venerable Abu Bakr admonished the impetuous younger man with the following words: "Is it Mohammad or the God of Mohammad that you worship? The God of Mohammad liveth for ever; but the apostle was a mortal like ourselves, and according to his own prediction, he has experienced the common fate of mortality."

It should be noted that the immediate successor of Mohammad, at the moment of his disappearance, called him an *apostle* instead of the Prophet. With the less ambitious designation of an apostle, Mohammad was placed by his followers on the level of other religious teachers and law-givers. Denial of the divinity of the Prophet made Islam the purest doctrine of Monotheism. Once divinity is conceded to a Prophet, before long, he assumes the attributes supposed to belong only to the Supreme Being. The unity of God or the absoluteness of the First Principle can no longer be maintained logically. Dubious theological devices endeavour to reconcile the contradiction. The original simplicity of faith is lost either in theological dogmatism or mystical self-deception. Without the severity of its theology, Islam could not claim the historic role as creditably as it did. When the Prophet is deprived of divinity, or his claim to it is not generally admitted, the scripture cannot command absolute and infallible authority. Consequently, a lattitude is left for the mind of the faithful. The teaching of a mortal cannot have the majesty of eternal truth, and scriptural laws cannot claim immutability.

Until the twelveth century, Islam did not possess a homogenous body of dogmas. Subject to the belief in one God, the Mussulman had a practically unlimited latitude for his spiritual life. And history shows that the Arabian thinkers made free and full use of that flexibility of the new faith. In order to refute the Christian doctrines of Trinity, which they considered to be a vulgarisation of the sublime idea of the Supreme God, Muslim theologists developed the fundamental idea of religion to the most abstract form ever conceived by human mind. (Vide Renan, "Averroes et Averroeism", p. 76). They could perform that unparallelled feat of theological rasiocination because "the Monotheism of Mohammad was the most absolute, and comparatively the freest from mythical adulterations." (F.A. Lange, "The History of Materialism," Vol. I, p. 184). The same authority testifies to the fact that the fundamental principles of religion laid down crudely by the founder of Islam were pregnant with the possibility of great development. And because of their rigid monotheistic nature, the development inevitably transcended the narrow limits of religious thought and culminated into a spiritual aflorescence which closed the age of faith. "Even before the communication of Greek philosophy to the Arabians, Islam had produced numerous sects and theological schools, some of which entertained so abstract a notion of God that no philosophical speculation could proceed farther in this direction, whilst others believed nothing but what could be understood and demonstrated;...... In the high school at Basra, there arose, under the protection of the Abbassides, a school of rationalists which sought to reconcile religion and faith." (Ibid., p. 177).

During the first five or six hundred years of its history, Islam produced not only scholars who occupied themselves more with heavenly bodies than with heavenly beings, who quietly set aside the Koran and placed greater spiritual value on the study of profane books, but revolutionary thinkers who ruthlessly sacrificed faith on the altar of reason. Not a few "Commanders of the Faithful" themselves—those who reigned at Bagdad, Kairo or Cordova until the eleventh century—attached greater value to positive knowledge than to revealed wisdom. The independent Empire of Bokhara preferred poets to the priests, doctors of medicine to doctors of divinity, and encouraged scientific research rather than the propagation of faith.

When we bear in mind that this line of intellectual development was opened up not only by the socio-political conditions created by the triumph of Islam, but originated in the central dogma of Mohammad's religion, neither the curiosities of the Koran nor the primitiveness of the Islamic faith should permit us to underestimate the historical role of Islam.

CHAPTER SIX.

ISLAMIC PHILOSOPHY.

THE age of Arabian learning lasted about five hundred years, and coincided with the darkest period of European history During the same period, India also was lying prostrate, under the triumphant Brahmanical reaction which had subverted or corrupted Buddhism. Eventually, it was, thanks to the inglorious success of having overcome the Buddhist revolution, that India fell such an easy prey to Muslim invaders.

Under the enlightened reign of the Abbassides, the Fatemites and the Ommiades rulers, learning and culture prospered respectively in Asia, North-Africa and Spain. From Samarkand and Bokhara to Fez and Cordova, numerous scholars studied and taught astronomy, mathematics, physics, chemistry, medicine and music. The invaluable treasure of Greek philosophy and learning had been buried under the intolerance and superstition of the Christian Church. Had it not been for the Arabs, it would have been irretrivably lost, and the dire consequence of such a mishap can be easily imagined.

Vain piety and hypocritical holiness induced the Christians to spurn the science of antiquity as profane. In consequence of that vanity of ignorance, the peoples of Europe were plunged into the mediæval darkness which threatened to be bottomless and interminable. The happy resurrection of the divine light of knowledge, lit by the sages of ancient Greece, at long last dissippated the depressing darkness of ignorance and superstition, prejudice and intolerance, and showed the European peoples the way to material prosperity, intellectual progress and spiritual liberation. It was through the Arabian philosophers and scientists that the rich patrimony of Greek learning reached the fathers of modern rationalism and the pioneer of scientific research, Roger Bacon, was a disciple of the Arabs. In the opinion of Humboldt, the Arabians are to be considered "the proper founders of the physical sciences, in the signification of the term which we are now accustomed to give it." ("Kosmos", Vol. II.) Experiment and measurement are the great instruments with the aid of which they made a path for progress, and raised themselves to a position of the connecting link between the scientific achievements of the Greek and those of the modern time.

Al Kandi, Al Hassan, Al Farabi, Avicena, Al Gazali, Abubakr, Avempace, Al Phetragius. (The Arabian names are so contracted in historical works written in European languages)—these are names memorable in the annals of human culture; and the fame of the great Averroes has been immortalised as that of the man who made the forerunners of modern civilisation acquainted with the genius of Aristotle, thereby giving an inestimable impetus to the struggle of the European humanity to liberate itself from the paralysing influence of theological bigotry and sterile scholasticism. The epoch-making role of the great Arab rationalist, who flourished in the first half of the twelveth century under the enlightened patronage of the Sultan of Andalusia, is eloquently depicted by the well-known saying of Roger Bacon: "Nature was interpreted by Aristotle, and Aristotle interpreted by Averroes."

The standard of spiritual revolt against the authority of the Christian Church, and the domination of theology, was hoisted in the thirteenth and fourteenth centuries. The rationalist rebels drew their inspiration from the scientific teachings of the great philosophers of ancient Greece, and these they learned from the Arabian scholars, particularly Averroes.

The bigotry of the pious Justinian, in the beginning of the sixth century, finally purged the holy world of Christian superstition of the remaining vestiges of pagan learning. The last Greek scholars were forced to leave the ancient seats of learning. They emigrated from the Roman Empire, and sought refuge in Persia; but there also sacredotal intolerance proved equally hostile to profane learning. Eventually, the derelict science of Athenian culture found a hospitable home in the court of the Abbassides Khalifs of Bagdad who were so impressed by the wisdom of those foreign infidels that neither Koran, nor sword was offered to them. On the contrary, all the remaining votaries of ancient learning, whose knowledge ridiculed faith, and indulgently smiled at all religion, were invited to accept the liberal hospitality of the Commander of the faithful.

The Khalifs not only took the exiled Greek scholars under their protection. They dispatched competent men to different parts of the Roman Empire with the instruction and the means to collect all the available works of the sages of ancient Greece. The precious works of Aristotle, Hipparchus, Hyppocrates, Galen and other scientists were translated into the Arabian language, and the Khalifs gave every encouragement to the propagation of those irreligious teachings throughout the Muslim world. Schools established at State expense disseminated scientific knowledge to thousands of students belonging to all classes of society,—"from the son of the noble to that of the mechanic". Poor students received education free, and teachers were handsomely remunerated for their services which were held at the highest esteem. The Arab historian, Abul Faragius, records the following views of Khalif Al Manon regarding the men of leaning: "They are the elect of God, his best and most useful servants, whose lives are devoted to the improvement of their rational faculties......The teachers of wisdom are the true luminaries and legislators of a world which without their aid would again sink into ignorance and barbarism.

The current notion of the bigotry and fanaticism of Islam loses all historical authenticity when it is known that the men of learning so highly appreciated by the successors of the Prophet, were mostly devoid of any religious fervour, not a few of them holding views frankly heretical; and the general burden of their teachings was the assertion of the reason of man as the only standard of truth. History does not provide the critical student with many instances of the head of a religious order encouraging the "improvement of rational faculties", as Khalif Al Manon did. For, the cultivation of rational faculties is entirely incompatible with faith. Yet, Al Manon was but one of the illustrious line of Abbassides Khalifs who not only encouraged the propagation of scientific knowledge, but themselves participated in it. Nor were the enlightened Abbassides an exception.

The Fatemites of Africa and the Omminades of Spain rivalled them in political power, material prosperity as well as in the patronage and propagation of knowledge. The library of Cairo contained over one hundred thousand volumes; whereas Cordova boasted of six times as many. This fact gives lie to another calumny which depicts the rise of Islam as an eruption of savage fanaticism, namely, the tale of the destruction of the famous library of Alexandria. One must have a pious mind or credulous disposition to believe that those who took delight in founding and supporting such noble seats of learning, would have callously set fire to the library of Alexandria; that those who command the gratitude of mankind for having saved its most precious patrimony, could have possibly begun by contributing to the destruction of that treasure. When dispassionate and scientific study of history dissipates legends and discredits malicious tales, the rise of Islam stands out not as a scourge but a blessing for the mankind.

While books written in the eleventh and twelvth century indignantly detail the shocking tale of the burning of the library of Alexandria, the historians Eustichius and Elmacin, both Egyptian Christians, who wrote soon after the Saracen conquest of their country, are significantly silent about the savage act. The former, a patriarch of Alexandria, could be hardly suspected of partiality to the enemies of Christianity. An order of Khalif Omar has been usually cited as evidence of the barbarous act ascribed to his general. It would have been much easier not to record that order than to suppress any historical work composed by Christian prelates who had endless possibilities of concealing their composition. A diligent examination of all relevant evidence enabled Gibbon to arrive at the following opinion on the matter: "The rigid sentence of Omar is repugnant to the sound and orthodox precept of the Mohammadan Casuits; they expressly declare that the religious books of the Jews and Christians, which are acquired by the right of war, should never be committed to the flames, and that the works of profane scientists, historians or poets, physicians or philosophers, may be lawfully applied to the use of the faithful." ("Rise and Fall of the Roman Empire").

Since history began to be written with impartial criticism, the tale of the destruction of the Alexandrian library has either been discredited or subjected to grave doubt. In any case, at the time of the Saracen conquest, the library of Alexandria had ceased to be the repository of the valuable records of Greek learning. Long before that time, Alexandria had enshrined Christian bigotry in the place of scientific knowledge and philosophical wisdom. The character of the contents of the library must have changed accordingly. The pagan scholars, driven by Christian intolerance away from the seat of ancient learning, must have carried away the treasures they valued more than all other things. If the flame was actually lit by the order of Omar, it consumed ponderous tomes of theological controversy which had done immensely more harm than good to mankind. The fire of Islam might have consumed the none too precious records of vain and futile theological disputations; but the admirable ardour the free-thinking Khalifs collected, preserved and improved the valuable records of ancient learning which had left the Alexandrian library before its useless and pernicious contents were put to the flames.

Byzantine barbarism had undone the meritorious work of the Ptolymies. The real destruction of the Alexandrian seat of learning had been the work of St. Cyril who defiled the Goddess of learning in the famous fair of Hyparia. That was already in the beginning of the fifth century. The Christian Saint would not tolerate that philosophical lectures and mathematical discourses held by a young pagan woman should be patronised by the elite of Alexandrian society, while the pious but incomprehensible sermons of the Archbishop were attended only by the rebels. If he was no match intellectually, he possessed the power to eliminate competition once for all. Under his instigation, the rebels, led by a regiment of monks burning with religious frenzy, attacked the seat of Alexandrian learning and, in the name of religion, perpetrated crimes too painful to be recorded and too shameful to be remembered.

"Thus, in the four hundred and fourteenth year of our era, the position of philosophy in the intellectual metropolis of the world was determined; henceforth, science must sink into obscurity and subordination. Its public existence will no longer be tolerated. Indeed, it may be said that from this period for some centuries it altogether disappeared. The leaden mace of bigotry had struck and shivered the exquisitely tempered steel of Greek philosophy. Cyril's act passed unquestioned. It was now ascertained that throughout the Roman world, there must be no more liberty of thought....Such assertions might answer their purposes very well so long as the victors maintained their power in Alexandria, but they manifestly are of inconvenient application after the Saracens had captured the city...... For the next two dreary and weary centuries, things remained, until oppression and force were ended by foreign invaders. It was well for the world that the Arabian conquerors avowed their true argument, the scimitar, and made no pretensions to superhuman wisdom. They were thus left free to pursue knowledge without involving themselves in theological contradictions, and were able to make Egypt once more illustrious among the nations of the earth,—to snatch it from the hideous fanaticism, ignorance and barbarism into which it had been plunged." (Draper, "The History of the Intellectual Development of Europe," Vol. 1, p. 325).

The works of the sages of ancient Greece were not only rescued, collected and preserved by the Arabs. They were profusely commented and improved upon. Complete works of Plato, Aristotle, Euklid, Appolonius, Ptolemy, Hyppocrates and Galen were available to the fathers of modern Europe at first only in Arabic versions, accompanied by erudite commentaries. Modern Europe learned from the Arabs not only medicine and mathematics. The science of astronomy, which widens the vision of man and reveals before him the mechanical laws of nature, was jealously cultivated by the Arabs. With the aid of new instruments of observation, Arab philosophers acquired exact knowledge about the circumference of the earth the position and number of planets. In their hand, astronomy began to outgrow its primitive form, (devinations of Astrology), cultivated more or less by the priests of all Oriental countries, and to develop into an exact science. Although algebra had been invented by Diophantus of Alexandria, it did not become an object of common study until the age of Arabic learning. As a matter of fact, the name of the science has given currency to the theory of its Arabian origin. But the Arabs themselves modestly acknowledged their indebtness to the Greek master. Botany was studied for medical purposes; yet the discovery of two thousand varieties of plants by Dioscorides represented the birth of a new science. Alchimy was a secret, jealously guarded by the priests of ancient Egypt. It was also practiced at Babylon. In a much later period, rudiments of chemistry were also known to the physicians of India. But the science of chemistry owes its origin and initial developments to the industry of the Arabs. "They first invented and named the alembic for the purposes of distillation; analysed the substances of the three kingdoms of nature; tried the distinction and affinities of alkalis and acids; and converted the precious minerals into soft and salutary medicine." (Gibbon).

It was in the science of medicine that the Arabs made the greatest progress. Masua and Geber were worthy disciples of Galen, and substantially added to what they had learned from the great master. Avicena, born in distant Bokhara, in the tenth century, reigned in Europe as the undisputed authority of the medical science for five hundred years. The school of Salermo, until the sixteenth century, was the centre of medical learning in Europe. It owed its origin to the Saracens and taught the lessons of Avicena.

The distinctive merit of the Arab scholars was the zeal to acquire knowledge through observation. They discarded the vanity of airy speculation, and stood firmly on the ground known to them. That great merit of Arabian learning is decisively evidenced in the following view of its Doyen Averroes: "The religion peculiar to philosophers is the study of that which is; for no sublimer worship can be given to God than the knowledge of his works, which leads to the knowledge of him and his reality. That is the noblest action in His eyes; the vilest is taxing, as error and vain presumption, the efforts of those who practise this worship, and who in this religion have the purest of religions." A religion which permitted the propagation of such irreligious views, though garbed in a pious phraseology, could not have its origin in intolerance and fanaticism. For this heterodox view, the philosopher, of course, incurred the wrath of the priesthood; but much more of the Christian than the Muslim.

After a short banishment, Averroes was restituted in his position in the court of the Sultan of Andalusia, and his books survived proscription in the Islamic world. But from their Latin version, the above and similar passages were expunged. Yet, the heretic movements of Europe, during the twelveth, thirteenth and fourteenth century, drew their inspiration from the suppressed teachings of the Arab philosopher; and it was the heretic movement that shook the foundation of the Catholic Church which had held Europe in spiritual subordination throughout the middle-ages. From the twelveth century onwards, until the triumph of modern learning, Averroism was analogous to heresy in the horrified eye of Christian holiness. And it was for nothing that it was so. For, alone the passage quoted above indicated the surest point of departure for the quest of positive knowledge which eventually cleared away the debris of ignorance, sanctified as faith, and glorified as virtue on the authority of theological dogmas.

In this passage, Averroes stated the

basic principle of the inductive method—the surest way to true knowledge. On the preconceived notion of a creator is set aside, and of is made to *know* him (as distinct from the blind faith in his existence) in his reality through the empirical knowledge of his works, that is, nature, the divine object recedes farther and farther, until it vanishes into nothingness,— the only demonstrable reality about his existence; and a religion which promoted that singular quest for the knowledge of God certainly represented the greatest advance of human ideology under the garb of religion. The latest of Great Religions, Islam was the greatest; and as such destroyed the basis of all religions. That is the essence of its historical significance.

The centre of Islam and Arabic learning was in those very historical regions where the older civilisations of the Egyptians, Assyrians, Jews, Persians and Greeks had arisen, clashed and fallen. The positive outcome of those earlier civilisations went into the making of the Arabian culture, and the remarkable Monotheism of Mohammad made its own the cardinal principles of the religion of those ancient peoples. It stands to the credit of the Arabian philosophers that they, for the first time, conceived the sublime idea of a common origin of all religions. Not only did they hold the view, singularly broad for the epoch, that all religions were so many efforts of the human mind to solve the great mysteries of life and nature; they went so much farther as to make the bold suggestion that the effort more reconcilable with reason was the greater, nobler and sublimer. This rationalistic view of religion attained the highest clarity in the mind of Averroes.

Thus, together with the invaluable metaphysical and scientific teachings of the sages of Athens and Alexandria, the Arabs contributed something original to the foundation of modern civilisation. It was scepticism—that powerul solvent of all faith. As soon as criticism challenges credulity, a new light dawns on the perspective of human progress. A curious book, anonymously published with the title "Three Imposters", occupies a prominent place in the early history of scepticism in Europe. The credit for that scandalous composition was attributed either to the heretical Christian Emperor Frederic Barbarossa, or the Muslim philosopher Averroes: The imposters were Moses, Christ and Mohammad. One of the suspected authors was a Chriistian and the other was a Mussulman. Religion certainly had fallen in bad days.

There had been scepticism before the thirteenth century, but no real incredulity. This doctrine and that had been disputed or rejected; but the foundation of Christian faith had never been touched. It was this foundation which was assailed when the idea was conceived that all religions have a common ground. If all religions are essentially the same, then the doctrine and dogmas peculiair to each other should be discarded as pernicious obstacles to the realisation of the spiritual unity of mankind. But freed from doctrines and dogmas, religion has no leg to stand upon. Its rationalisation amounts to its destruction. The revolutionary idea of the common origin of all religions was conceived for the first time by the Arab thinkers.

Although Arabian learning reached its climax in Averroes, he was but the greatest and the latests of a long succession of great thinkers and scholars who flourished from the ninth to the thirteenth century. A brief reference to the substance of the teachings of the more illustrious of them will give some idea of the revolutionary significance of the learning which owed its origin to the cardinal principle of the Mohammadan religion, and was promoted by the staggering achievements of the "Sword of God."

Having established unity, as the terrestrial reflection of their spiritual unitarianism, and promoted economic prosperity in consequence thereof, the new Islamic nation devoted itself to the culture of the mind. For a hundred years, it modestly learned from others, particularly the ancient Greeks. Thus equipped, it began to produce independent and original thought in every branch of learning.

Al Kandi was the earliest of the great Arabian philosophers. He flourished in the capital of the free-thinking Abbassides, and leaped into fame in the beginning of the nineth century. For teaching that philosophy must be based on mathematics; that is, it should cease to be idle speculation: abstract thought should be guided by precise reasoning, based on concrete facts and established laws, in order to produce positive results. The teacher of this doctrine deserves the great distinction of having anticipated Francis Bacon and Descartes by seven hundred years as a forerunner of modern philosophy. Even to-day there are many "philosophers" and scholars who could be profited by the wisdom taught by the Saracen sage a thousand years ago.

Next to be mentioned is Al Farabi who lived in the following century, and taught at Damascus as well as Bagdad. His commentary on Aristotle was studied for centuries as an authoritative work on the subject. He also excelled in the medical science. Roger Bacon. learned mathematics from him.

In the latter half of the tenth century appeared Avicena. He belonged to a rich landowning family of Bokhara engaged in prosperous trade. He wrote on mathematics and physics, but went down in history for his contributions to the medical science.

The famous medical school of Salermo was a monument to his memory, and his work was the text book of medicine throughout Europe until the sixteenth century. The great physician's philosophical views were so unorthodox that even the free-thinking Emir of Bokhara could not resist the pressure of the Imams who were scandalised by the profanity of Avicena. He had to leave the court of his patron, and travelled all over the Arabic Empire teaching medicine and preaching his philosophy at different seats of learning.

In the eleventh century lived Al Hassan who deserves a place among the greatest scientists of all ages. Optics was his special subject. Having learned it from the Greeks, he went farther than they, who corrected their mistaken notion that the rays of light issue from the eye. By anatomical and geometrical reasoning, Al Hassan proved that the rays of light came from the object seen, and impinged on the retina. There is ground for belief, held by many historians of science, that Keppler borrowed his optical views from his Arab predecessor.

In the same century also lived Al Gazali, son of an Andalusian merchant. He anticipated Descartes in reducing the standard of truth to self-consciousness. He stands out as the connecting link between the antique and modern scepticism. His memorable contribution to philosophy is better stated in his own words: "Having failed to get satisfaction from religion, I finally resolved to discard all authority, and detach myself from opinions which have been instilled in me during the unsuspecting years of childhood. My aim is simply to know the truth of things; consequently it is indispensable for me to ascertain what is knowledge. Now it was evident to me that certain knowledge must be that which explains the object to be known in such a manner that no doubt can remain, so that in future all error and conjecture respecting it must be impossible. Thus, once I have acknowledged ten to be more than three, if any one were to say: "On the contrary, three is more than ten; and to prove my assertion I will change this stick into a serpent; and if he actually did the miracle, still my conviction of his error would remain unshaken. His manoeuvre would only produce in me admiration for his ability, but I should not doubt my own knowledge."

The principle of acquiring exact knowledge, stated nearly a thousand years ago, by the Muslim savant, still holds as good as then; and the scientific outlook which makes such knowledge possible, is still comparatively rare among the Indians, who even in these days of the twentieth century allow themselves to be imposed by feats of magic and "spiritual" charlatanism, and credit these as serious challenge to the reliability of scientific knowledge.

Al Gazali held that knowledge could not possess such mathematical exactness, unless it were acquired empirically, and governed by irrefragible laws established by experience. He was of the opinion that incontestable conviction could be acquired only through sense perceptions, and necessary truth, that is, casualty. In reason (self-consciousness) he found the judge of the correctness of the perception of senses.

One is amazed to find such unique boldness of thought in the atmosphere of a religion generally believed to be the most intolerant and fanatical. Yet, Al Gazali's scepticism was avidly studied throughout the Muslim world of his time. His place in the history of philosophy can be judged from the opinion of the famous French Orientalist Renan, who thought that the father of modern scepticism, Hume, did not say anything more than what had been said by the Arab philosopher who preceded him by seven hundred years. The immensity of the historical significance of Al Gazali's views is appreciated still more clearly when we remember that it was scepticism of Hume which gave impetus to Kant's "all shattering critical philosophy" that laid a cruel axe at the root of all speculative thought. But Al Gazali's views were a long way ahead of time. Experimental science, as he visualised, was not yet possible. In the absence or infancy of technology, the nature of objects could not be so mathematically ascertained as the philosophers wished. Therefore, in his later years, Al Gazali fell into mysticism; but his fall was not more strikingly inglorious than of Kant. Objective drawbacks clipped the intrepid wings of the soaring spirit of the Arab thinker; whereas subjective predilection of class interest overwhelmed the critical genius of Kant.

Abubakr, who lived in the twelfth century, was the first astronomer to reject the Ptolemic notion regarding the position of heavenly bodies. He conceived of a planetary system, and celestial motion which tended towards the epoch-making discoveries of Giordano Bruno, Galileo and Copernicus. It is recorded that "in his systems all movements were verified, and therefore no error resulted." Abubakr dies before having set forth his theory in a complete treatise. His pupil, Al Phetragius, popularised his teaching that all planetary bodies moved regularly. Throughout the middle-ages, the hypothesis was valued as a great contribution to astronomical knowledge. The teachings of a Muslim philosopher, which upset the biblical view of the Universe, penetrated the Christian monasteries. Not only Roger Bacon, but his illustrious opponent, Albertus Magnus, also acknowledged the indebtedness to the astronomical work of Al Phetragius in which Abubakr's views on planetary movement were expounded.

The basic principle of the philosophy of Averroes, the greatest and the latest of the great Arabian thinkers, have already been outlined. He lived at the turning point of the history of the Islamic culture. By the twelfth century, the pinacle had been reached, and the forces of reaction had gathered strength to overwhelm those of progress. Islamic culture was already on the decline

The freedom of thought permitted by the simple faith of a nomadiic people, had attained such soaring heights of boldness as eventually clashed with the temporal interests of the "Commanders of the Faithful." When the positive outcome of Islamic thought, developed so marvellously during five hundred years, was summarised in the highly revolutionary dictum of Averroes that reason is the only source of truth, Sultan Al Masur of Cordova, under the pressure of the priests, issued an edict condemning such heretical views to hell-fire, on the authority of religion. The denunciation of the noblest product of Islam naturally marked the beginning of its degeneration from a powerful lever of human progress to an instrument of reaction, intolerance, ignorance and prejudice. Having played out its historic role—to rescue the precious patrimony of ancient culture out of the engulfing ruins of two Empires and the blinding darkness of two religions—Islam turned traitor to its original self, and became the black banner of Turkish barbarism and of the depredations of the Mongolian herds.

Islam disownned its own. Averroes was driven away from the court of Cordova—the home of free thought for centuries. His books were condemned to the flames, if not actually of fire, to those of the more merciless sacredotal reaction. Rationalism came to be identified with heresy. The very names of Averroes and his master, Aristotle, became anathema. In course of time, reaction triumphed so completely that for an orthodox Mohammadan, philosophy stood for "infidelity, impiety, and immoralitiy." But the standard of spiritual progress, admirably held high, and boldly carried forward by the Arabs during five hundred years, could not be lowered and trampled under the fury of vain religiosity any more successfully by Islamic inntolerance than previously by Christian piety and superstition. Averroes was diowned by his own people, only to be enthroned by those to whom belonged the future. The fierce contest between Faith and Reason, between despotic ignorance and freedom of thought, which rocked Europe and shook the foundation of the Catholic Church from the twelfth century onwards, drew inspiration from the teachings of the Arab philosophers. Averroes and Averroism dominated the scientific thought of Europe for four hundred years.

CHAPTER SEVEN.

ISLAM AND INDIA.

ALTHOUGH Islam came to India after it had played out its progressive role, and its leadership had been wrested from the learned and cultured Arabs, the revolutionary principles of the days of its origin and ascendency were still inscribed on its flag; and a critical study of history might reveal that the Muslim conquest of India was facilitated by similar native factors as in the case of Persia and the Christian countries. No great people, with a long history and old civilisation, can ever succumb easily to a foreign invasion, unless the invaders command the sympathy and acquiescence, if not active support, of the masses of the conquered people. Brahmanical orthodoxy having overwhelmed the Buddhist revolution, India of the eleventh and twelveth centuries must have been infested with multitudes of persecuted heretics who would eagerly welcome the message of Islam.

Mohammad Ibn Kassim conquered Sindh with the active assistance of the Jats and other agricultural communities oppressed by the Brahman rulers. Having conquered the country, he followed the policy of the early Arab conquerors. "He employed the Brahmans in pacifying the country by taking them into confidence. He allowed them to repair their temples and to follow their own religion as before, placed the collection of revenue in their hands, and employed them in continuing the traditional system of local administration." (Elliot, "History of India) when even the Brahmans, some of them at any rate, were prepared to go over to the side of the *mlechha* conquerors, the social conditions of the country could not be very normal. Evidently, society was in such a disintegrated and chaotic state as to make the position even of the most privileged class insecure. That is usually the result of counter-revolution. A revolution may be defeated by a combination of forces; but that does not enable the triumphant forces of reaction to remove the causes of social disintegration which brought about the revolution. In India, the Buddhist revolution was not defeated; it was miscarried owing to its internal weakness. Social forces were not sufficiently mature to carry the revolution to victory. Consequently, after the downfall of Buddhism, the country found itself in a worse state of economic ruin, political oppression, intellectual anarchy and spiritual chaos. Practically, the entire society was involved in that tragic process of decay and decomposition. That is why not only the oppressed masses readily rallied under the banner of Islam which offered them social equality if not political liberty; even the upper classes offered their services to the foreign aggressor out of selfish motives. That shows that, while the masses were in a state of despair, the upper classes were thouroughly demoralised.

As regards the spread of Islam in India, an ardent admirer of ancient Hindu culture like Havell, who cannot be suspected of any sympathy or even fairness to the Muslims, gives the following highly interesting testimoney: "Those who did so (embraced Islam) acquired all the rights of a Musalman citizen in the law courts, where the Quran and not Aryan law and custom decided dispute in all cases. This method of proselytism was very effective among the lower castes of Hindus, specially among those who suffered from the severity of Brahmanical law with regard to the 'impure' classes." ("Aryan Rule in India.")

This is certainly not a very complimentary remark wrung from a firm believer in the perfection of Brahmanical law. In any case, it is clear that in the time of Mohammadan conquest, there lived in India multitudes of people who had little reason to be faithful to Hindu laws and the traditions of Brahman orthodoxy, and were ready to forsake that heritage for the more equitable laws of Islam which offered them protection against the tyranny of triumphant Hindu reaction.

In another place, Havell chooses to deprecate the spiritual values of the teachings of the Arabian Prophet. But at the same time makes a very significant statement regarding the spread of those teachings in India. "It was not the philosophy of Islam, but its sociological programme, which won so many converts for it in India." Of course, for the masses philosophy has no appeal. They are always attracted by a "sociological programme" which offers them something better than the given conditions of their life. And a bad philosophy, that is to say, a reactionary outlook of life, cannot be associated with a sociological programme which secures the support of the downtrodden masses. If the sociological programme of Islam found support of the Indian masses, it was because the philosophy behind that programme was better than the Hindu philosophy which had been responsible for the social chaos from which Islam showed a way out for the masses of the Indian people. By the above statement, Havell admits that even in the thirteenth and fourteenth centuries, when Islam was winning adherence in India, it had not altogether played out its social-revolutionary role, and that it was by virtue of its social-revolutionary character that it struck so deep a root in India. That is to say even in its days of degeneration and decay, Islam represented spiritual, ideological and social progress in relation to Hindu conservatism.

Havell is a famous eulogist of Indo-European culture which he considers to be the noblest product of the creative genius of man. On the other hand, he has bitter antipathy for the Muslims. His opinion cannot be dismissed as biassed against the Hindus. As a matter of fact, his bias is entirely on the side of the Hindus. So, if even a historian like him found distasteful things happening in India in the past, conditions were very deplorable indeed. He writes: "But the victorious progress of

Islam in India is not to be accounted for by external reasons. It was mainly due to the political degeneration of *Aryavarta* which set in after the death of Harsha....... The social programme of the Prophet...... gave every true believer an equal spiritual status ......made Islam a political and social synthesis and gave it an imperial mission.. Islam was a rule of life sufficient for the happiness of average humanity content to take the world as it is...... Islam reached the zenith of its political strength at the critical period when the conflict between Buddhist philosophy and that of orthodox Brahaminism was a potent cause of political dissension in northern India." (Ibid).

King Harshavardhan died in the middle of the seventh century. Thus, the political disintegration of India was a process parallel to the rise of Islam. The death of a king, however great, does not mark the turning point of history. The process had been going on for many centuries. The Buddhist revolution arrested it for a time, only to be aggravated, accentuated and accelerated on its defeat. Indeed, the monastic degeneration of Buddhism and its disintegrating influence on the entire Indian society greatly helped the Muslim conquest just as Christian monasticism had done elsewhere.

Commenting on Mahmud of Guzni's invasions, Havell further writes: "The almost invariable success of his arms added immensely to his prestige and brought Islam many adherents among the uncultured warrior classes of the North-Western Provinces to whom fighting was a religion and victory in the field the highest proof of inspiration." (Ibid). Mahmud's exploit could not but deal a staggering blow to the faith in the divinity of the shrines where the Indians had brought their offerings from times immemorial. Consequently, the religious feeling which found expression in the worship at the shrines, and the faith in their presiding deities were rudely shocked and inevitably shaken. In such circumstances, "religious feelings and spiritual instincts" induced the masses to transfer their devotion from the gods of demonstrated impotence to the more mighty one, the belief in, and worship for whom, incidentally, was rewarded so magnificently. For ages, millions had believed in the supernatural power of the gods worshipped at the famous temples of Thaneswar, Muttra, Somnath etc. The priests of those temples had amassed fabulous riches at the expense of the believing multitude by virtue of their pretensions to the ability of invoking the protection of the powerful divinities. Suddenly, the whole venerable structure of belief and tradition collapsed like a house of cards under the cruel blow of the invading infidel. When Mahmud's hosts approached, the priests told the people that the invaders would be devoured by the fiery wrath of the gods. The people confidently expected a miracle which failed to happen. Indeed, it was performed by the God of the invader. Being based upon miracle, faith necessarily is transfered to the most miraculous. Judged by all the traditional standards of religion, those who embraced Islam at that crisis were the most religious.

A critical investigation of the internal as well as the external causes of the Muslim conquest of India is of practical value today. It will remove the prejudice that makes the orthodox Hindu look upon his Muslim neighbour as an inferior being. Freed from preconceived ideas, the Hindus will be in a position to appreciate the constructive consequences of the Muslim conquest of India. That will enable them to live down the hatred of the conquered for the conquerors. Unless a radical change of attitude is brought about by a sober sense of history, the communal question will never be solved. The Hindus will never be able to look upon the Muslims as integral parts of the Indian nation until they come to appreciate the contribution they made towards the emergence of Indian society out of the chaos caused by the breakdown of the antique civilisation. Besides, a proper understanding of history derived from a correct understanding of the successful advent of the Muslims in India will enable us to ascertain and stamp out the deeper causes of our present misfortune.

On the other hand, few Muslims of our days may be conscious of the glorious role played on the stage of history by the faith they profess. Many may disown and repudiate the rationalism and scepticism of the Arabs as deviations from the teachings of the Koran. But Islam occupies a memorable place in history thanks rather to its original-unorthodoxy and irreligiosity made evident by the Arab philosophers, than to the later growth of a reactionary priesthood or to the barbarous fanaticism of the Tartar converts. Islam had played out its progressive role before it penetrated India. Its flag was planted on the banks of the Indus and the Ganges not by revolutionary Saracen heroes, but by Persians demoralised by luxury and the barbarians of Central Asia who had embraced Islam, both had suverted the Arab

Empire—that magnificent monument to the memory of Mohammad. Still, it was welcomed as a message of hope and freedom by the multitudinous victims of the Brahmanical reaction which had overthrown the Buddhist revolution and had consequently thrown the Indian society in a state of chaos. Neither the Persians nor the Mogul conquerors of India were entirely devoid of the traditional nobility, toleration and liberalism of the Saracen heroes. The very fact that comparatively small bands of predatory invaders from distant lands could make themselves the rulers of a vast country for such a long time, and their alien faith found millions of converts, proves that they did satisfy certain objective requirements of the Indian society. Even when much of its original revolutionary fervour had been overwhelmed by reaction, Islam still exercised certain revolutionary influence on the Hindu society. The Mohammadan power was consolidated in India not so much by the valour of the invaders' arms as owing to the propagation of the Islamic faith and the progressive significance of Islamic laws.

Even the fiercely fanatical anti-Muslim Havell grudgingly admits: "The effect of the Mussalman political creed upon Hindu social life was twofold: It increased the rigour of the casste system and aroused a revolt against it. The alluring prospect which it held out to the lower strata of Hindu society was as tempting as it was to the Beduins of the desert "....(It) made the *Sudra* a free man and potentially a lord of the Brahmans. Like the Renaissance of Europe, it stirred up the intellectual waters, produced many strong men, and some men of striking originality of genius. Like the Renaissance also, it was essentially a city cult; it made the nomads leave his tent and the *Sudra* abandon his village. It developed a type of humanity full of *joie de vivre*...." ("Aryan Rule in India").

To the above highly illuminating statement, it may only be added that the rise of reformers like Kabir, Nanak, Tukaram, Chaitanya, etc. who evidenced a popular revolt against Brahmanical orthodoxy, was to a great extent promoted by the social effects of Mohammadan conquest.

In view of this realistic reading of history, Hindu superciliousness towards the religion and culture of the Muslims is absurd. It insults history and injures the political future of our country. Learning from the Muslims, Europe became the leader of modern civilisation. Even to-day, her best sons are not ashamed of the past indebtedness. Unfortunately, India could not be fully benefitted by the heritage of Islamic culture, because she did not deserve the distinction. Now, in the throes of a belated Renaissance, Indians, both Hindus and Muslims, could profitably draw inspiration from that memorable chapter of human history. Knowledge of Islam's contribution to human cultured and proper appreciation of the historical value of that contribution would shock the Hindus out of their arrogant self-satisfaction, and cure the narrow-mindedness of the Muslims of our day by bringing them face to face with the true spirit of the faith they profess.